W9-DFU-902

TEAM SPIRIT®

SMART BOOKS FOR YOUNG FANS

# THE OAKLAND ATHLETICS

BY

MARK STEWART

NorwoodHouse Press
CHICAGO, ILLINOIS

Norwood House Press
P.O. Box 316598
Chicago, Illinois 60631

For information regarding Norwood House Press, please visit our website at:
www.norwoodhousepress.com or call 866-565-2900.

All photos courtesy of Getty Images except the following:
SportsChrome (4, 10), Goudey Gum Co. (6, 7, 17),
Black Book Partners Archive (9, 23, 26, 35 bottom right & top, 39, 43 top), Tom DiPace (11, 14),
Topps, Inc. (15, 22, 26, 35 bottom left, 40, 45), Williams Baking (16),
Author's Collection (24, 27, 31, 34 both, 41), Fun Foods, Inc. (33), Exhibit Supply Co. (37),
Bowman Gum Co. (42 top), SSPC (42 bottom), Sweet Caporal (43 bottom), Matt Richman (48).
Cover Photo: J. Meric/Getty Image

The memorabilia and artifacts pictured in this book are presented for educational and informational purposes, and come from the collection of the author.

Editor: Mike Kennedy
Designer: Ron Jaffe
Project Management: Black Book Partners, LLC.
Special thanks to Topps, Inc.

Library of Congress Cataloging-in-Publication Data

Stewart, Mark, 1960-
The Oakland Athletics / by Mark Stewart.
p. cm. -- (Team spirit)
Includes bibliographical references and index.
Summary: "A Team Spirit Baseball edition featuring the Oakland Athletics that chronicles the history and accomplishments of the team. Includes access to the Team Spirit website, which provides additional information, updates and photos"--Provided by publisher.
ISBN 978-1-59953-491-6 (library : alk. paper) -- ISBN 978-1-60357-371-9 (ebook) 1. Oakland Athletics (Baseball team)--History--Juvenile literature. I. Title.
GV875.O24S84 2012
796.357'640979466--dc23

2011048176



Manufactured in the United States of America in North Mankato, Minnesota.
196N—012012

**COVER PHOTO**: The A's exchange high-fives after a victory in 2011.

# TABLE OF CONTENTS

## ABOUT OUR GLOSSARY

In this book, there may be several words that you are reading for the first time. Some are sports words, some are new vocabulary words, and some are familiar words that are used in an unusual way. All of these words are defined on page 46. Throughout the book, sports words appear in **bold type**. Regular vocabulary words appear in ***bold italic type***.

A's
Athletics
4
G
SERIES

# MEET THE A'S

Usually in baseball, when one team finds a winning formula, other clubs try to do the same thing. The Oakland Athletics (or A's, for short) like to be ***unique***. They search for talent where other teams never think to look. They do things that make opponents scratch their heads. And when other teams try to copy the A's, they rarely do it as well.

That has been true for a very long time—longer than the team has been playing in California. Since the team started more than a century ago, the A's have been determined to do things their own way. As the old saying goes, you can't argue with success.

This book tells the story of the A's. They are one of baseball's longest-running success stories. The team is not afraid to try new things. But that's only part of the story. The A's also win because they know how to play baseball the old-fashioned way.

Coco Crisp gets a hand from coach Mike Gallego after a home run. Gallego was a member of Oakland's 1989 championship team.

# Glory Days

The A's have been playing on the west coast since moving to Oakland, California, in 1968. The team actually played its first season in 1901, as the Philadelphia Athletics, more than 2,000 miles away from its current home. Fans back then started calling the club the A's for short. The team's official name is still Athletics.

In their early days, the A's were among the best in the **American League (AL)**. They were managed for 50 years by Connie Mack, who built a winning foundation on pitching, defense, and base-stealing. Mack's first group of stars included Harry Davis, Frank Baker, Eddie Collins, Eddie Plank, Charles "Chief" Bender, and Rube Waddell. All are in the **Hall of Fame**, except for Davis.

During the 1920s, Mack rebuilt the A's as a power-hitting team. Sluggers such as Al Simmons and Jimmie Foxx competed with Babe Ruth and Lou Gehrig of the New York Yankees for the AL home run and **runs batted in (RBIs)** championships.

**LEFT**: This pennant dates back to the 1930s.
**RIGHT**: Al Simmons

Mickey Cochrane and Lefty Grove made up the best catcher-pitcher combination in baseball. Philadelphia won the **pennant** each year from 1929 to 1931. Grove was the first winner of the AL **Most Valuable Player (MVP)** Award, also in 1931.

After their great three-year run, the A's struggled for the rest of their time in Philadelphia. They had a few stars, including Bob Johnson, Wally Moses, Ferris Fain, Gus Zernial, and Bobby Shantz. However, by the end of the summer, the team was rarely in the pennant race.

After Mack retired, the A's moved to Kansas City, Missouri. They played there from 1955 to 1967, but they never had a winning season. In 1968, the A's moved farther west to Oakland. Many of the young players signed in Kansas City became stars in their new hometown. Catfish Hunter, Blue Moon Odom, Vida Blue, and Rollie Fingers

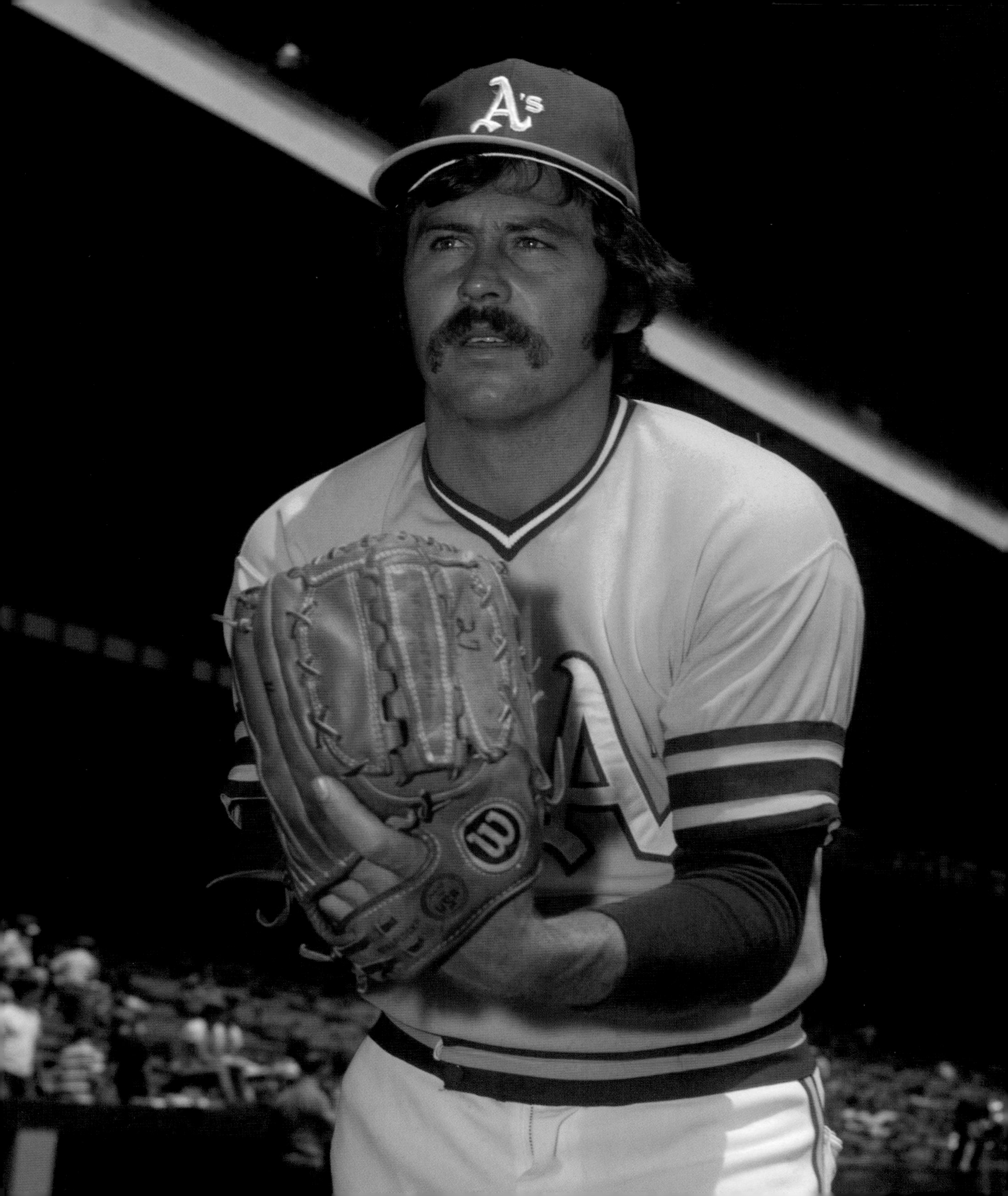
A's

helped the A's form the best pitching staff in the league. Reggie Jackson, Sal Bando, and Joe Rudi were the heart of a powerful offense.

The A's won the **World Series** three years in a row from 1972 to 1974. They were known as the "Moustache Gang" because the team's owner, Charles Finley, paid his players a bonus to grow moustaches. The team wore stunning green and gold uniforms during this time.

During the 1980s and 1990s, the A's kept playing exciting baseball. Rickey Henderson, Carney Lansford, Jose Canseco, and Mark McGwire were among the top hitters in baseball. Canseco became the first player with 40 homers and 40 steals in the same season. McGwire hit 49 home runs as a **rookie**. Pitchers Dave Stewart and

**LEFT**: Jim Hunter was better known to baseball fans as "Catfish."
**ABOVE**: Mark McGwire and Jose Canseco were nicknamed the "Bash Brothers."

Dennis Eckersley were at their best in big games. Oakland won three more pennants from 1988 to 1990.

As the stars of these great teams got older or were traded away, the A's needed to rebuild their club. They looked for young pitchers with the talent to become stars. Oakland discovered three aces in Tim Hudson, Mark Mulder, and Barry Zito. Each had a powerful arm and a wonderful understanding of pitching. Meanwhile, the A's also developed patient hitters with great power. Jason Giambi, Eric Chavez, and Nick Swisher led the charge.

From 1999 to 2006, the A's finished first or second in the **AL West** every year. Unfortunately, Oakland fell

**ABOVE**: Barry Zito **RIGHT**: Trevor Cahill

short of reaching the World Series. Soon it was time to find new stars to take the team into the future. The A's began the way they always do—adding strong-armed pitchers and hitters with a good batting eye. Young players such as Trevor Cahill, Brad Peacock, Josh Reddick, and Jemile Weeks joined the team. Their fans knew it wouldn't be long before the team was fighting for the AL West crown again.

AND ATHLETICS
A's

# Home Turf

When the Athletics played in Philadelphia, their home for most of those years was Shibe Park. It was later renamed Connie Mack Stadium in honor of the team's beloved manager. The A's played in Municipal Stadium after they moved to Kansas City. It was famous for its petting zoo, which was the home of the team's mascot, a mule named Charlie-O.

The A's moved into the Coliseum when they arrived in California in 1968. Pitchers love the stadium because it has a lot of room in foul territory for catching pop-ups. Hitters dislike it for the same reason. The Coliseum was originally built for the Oakland Raiders football team. The San Jose Earthquakes soccer team played there for two seasons, too.

## By the Numbers

- *The team's stadium has 35,067 seats for baseball.*
- *The distance from home plate to the left field foul pole is 330 feet.*
- *The distance from home plate to the center field fence is 400 feet.*
- *The distance from home plate to the right field foul pole is 330 feet.*

This view of Oakland's stadium shows the large amount of space in foul territory down the right field line.

A's

# DRESSED FOR SUCCESS

During their years in Philadelphia, the A's used blue and white as their team colors. In most years, the players wore a big letter *A* on their jerseys. Starting in 1929, their caps featured an *A*, too. The team was best known for its elephant ***logo***. After the Athletics moved to Kansas City, they spelled out their full name on their uniforms. Later, the letters *KC* replaced the *A* on the team's cap.

In the 1960s, the A's began wearing sleeveless tops. They also changed their team colors to green and gold and started using a capital *A* on their uniforms again. For some road games, they wore gold pants and tops.

In 1972, the A's switched to ***traditional*** uniform tops again. In 1988, the elephant reappeared on their sleeves. Today, the A's sometimes wear gold or green jerseys that remind fans of the team's past.

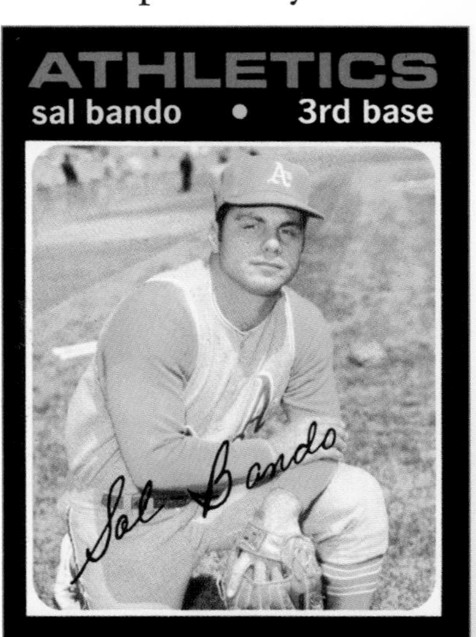


**LEFT**: Andrew Bailey wears the team's 2011 home uniform.
**ABOVE**: Sal Bando models a green and gold sleeveless uniform on his 1971 trading card.

When a team plays championship baseball over several seasons, fans sometimes call this a ***dynasty***. The A's have had four dynasties during their history. They won four pennants from 1910 to 1914, three pennants from 1929 to 1931, three pennants from 1972 to 1974, and three pennants from 1988 to 1990. In all, those teams were World Series winners nine times.

The first championship club for the A's featured base-stealer Eddie Collins and pitcher Jack Coombs. Philadelphia faced the Chicago Cubs in the World Series and defeated them easily. Coombs won three games. Collins hit .429 and stole four bases.

The A's won the World Series again in 1911. This time, they defeated the New York Giants four games to two. The hero for the A's was their hard-hitting third baseman, Frank Baker. He slammed dramatic home runs off New York's best pitchers to help the A's win two close games. Philadelphia beat the Giants again in the 1913 World Series. Baker and Chief Bender led the A's to victory, this time in five games.

The A's might have kept winning were it not for a new league called the **Federal League**. Many of the team's best players were offered more money to join the "Feds." Connie Mack could not afford to match those offers. It took 15 years before he was able to build another great team.

From 1929 to 1931, the A's ruled the AL. They beat the Cubs in the 1929 World Series and the St. Louis Cardinals in 1930. The Cardinals defeated the A's in 1931. Lefty Grove, Jimmie Foxx, Mickey Cochrane, and Al Simmons were the team leaders in those years. However, it was the great play of lesser-known A's such as Bing Miller, Howard Ehmke, and George Earnshaw that turned Philadelphia into a champion.

**LEFT**: This card of Connie Mack was printed after the 1910 championship.
**ABOVE**: Jimmie Foxx, Al Simmons, and Mickey Cochrane formed the heart of Mack's batting order in the 1920s and 1930s.

After moving to Oakland, the A's won three World Series in a row from 1972 to 1974. Those teams had great pitching, including Catfish Hunter, Vida Blue, Ken Holtzman, and Rollie Fingers. They also had good hitters, including Bert Campaneris, Sal Bando, Joe Rudi, and Reggie Jackson.

Jackson was injured and did not play in the 1972 World Series against the Cincinnati Reds. But Hunter beat the Reds twice, and a little-used catcher named Gene Tenace supplied all the power Oakland needed to win in seven games. Jackson was in good shape for the 1973 World Series against the New York Mets. He got the winning hits in Game 6 and Game 7. Fingers was the star in 1974 against the Los Angeles Dodgers—the first ever "all-California" World Series.

Oakland won three pennants in a row again from 1988 to 1990. Jose Canseco, Mark McGwire, Rickey Henderson, and Carney Lansford powered the Oakland offense. Dave Stewart, Bob Welch, and Dennis Eckersley were the team's top pitchers.

Oakland was defeated in the World Series in 1988 and 1990, but in 1989 the team swept the San Francisco Giants. The four games took 14 days to play because of an earthquake that struck both cities. Stewart and Henderson were the leading players for the A's. The Oakland victory was an impressive one—the team did not trail the Giants for a single inning.

**LEFT**: Reggie Jackson takes a mighty swing during the 1973 World Series.
**ABOVE**: The A's celebrate their championship in 1989.

# GO-TO GUYS

To be a true star in baseball, you need more than a quick bat and a strong arm. You have to be a "go-to guy"—someone the manager wants on the pitcher's mound or in the batter's box when it matters most. Fans of the A's have had a lot to cheer about over the years, including these great stars …

## THE PIONEERS

### EDDIE PLANK — Pitcher

• BORN: 8/31/1875 • DIED: 2/24/1926 • PLAYED FOR TEAM: 1901 TO 1914

Eddie Plank stepped toward first base when he pitched, then threw the ball across his body toward home plate. This "cross-fire" style confused most hitters. Plank won 20 or more games for the A's seven times.

### RUBE WADDELL — Pitcher

BORN: 10/13/1876 • DIED: 4/1/1914 • PLAYED FOR TEAM: 1902 TO 1907

Rube Waddell threw harder than any pitcher of his time. He led the AL in strikeouts every year he pitched for the A's and won more than 20 games four times. In his last three seasons in Philadelphia, he had 23 **shutouts**.

**RIGHT**: Lefty Grove

## AL SIMMONS — Outfielder

• BORN: 5/22/1902 • DIED: 5/26/1956

• PLAYED FOR TEAM: 1924 TO 1932, 1940 TO 1941 & 1944

No one played harder than Al Simmons. He was a powerful hitter, good fielder, and excellent baserunner. The right-handed Simmons used an extra-long bat because he stepped toward third base when he swung.

## MICKEY COCHRANE — Catcher

• BORN: 4/6/1903 • DIED: 6/28/1962 • PLAYED FOR TEAM: 1925 TO 1933

Catchers were not expected to be great hitters when Mickey Cochrane played. He made fans look at his position in a different way. From 1929 to 1931, Cochrane batted better than .340, and the A's won the pennant each year.

## LEFTY GROVE — Pitcher

• BORN: 3/6/1900 • DIED: 5/22/1975

• PLAYED FOR TEAM: 1925 TO 1933

Many experts believe that Lefty Grove was baseball's best pitcher during his years with the A's. He led the AL in strikeouts in each of his first seven seasons and had the lowest **earned run average (ERA)** in the league four years in a row.

## JIMMIE FOXX — First Baseman

• BORN: 10/22/1907 • DIED: 7/21/1967 • PLAYED FOR TEAM: 1925 TO 1935

Jimmie Foxx was one of the strongest sluggers in history. He once shattered a seat in the upper deck of Yankee Stadium. Another time, he hit a ball over the roof of Chicago's Comiskey Park. Foxx slammed 58 home runs in 1932 and won the **Triple Crown** in 1933.

## CATFISH HUNTER — Pitcher

• BORN: 4/8/1946 • DIED: 9/9/1999 • PLAYED FOR TEAM: 1965 TO 1974

The A's had many good pitchers in the 1970s, but Catfish Hunter was the best. He won 20 or more games four years in a row. Hunter had great control—he could throw any pitch to any spot at any time.

## REGGIE JACKSON — Outfielder

• BORN: 5/18/1946 • PLAYED FOR TEAM: 1967 TO 1975 & 1987

Reggie Jackson was the most exciting hitter of his time. When he unleashed his powerful swing, the ball either jumped off his bat or hissed right past him. Either way, Jackson brought the fans out of their seats.

## RICKEY HENDERSON — Outfielder

• BORN: 12/25/1958

• PLAYED FOR TEAM: 1979 TO 1984, 1989 TO 1995 & 1998

Rickey Henderson was a patient hitter who could draw a walk or smash the ball out of the park. Henderson was also a great base-stealer. In 1982, he set a record with 130 stolen bases. Henderson retired with the most steals (1,406) in baseball history.

## DENNIS ECKERSLEY Pitcher

• BORN: 10/3/1954

• PLAYED FOR TEAM: 1987 TO 1995

Dennis Eckersely was a 20-game winner as a young starter. He became a relief pitcher with the A's and led the league in **saves** twice. In 1992, "Eck" won the **Cy Young Award** and was named AL MVP.

## TREVOR CAHILL Pitcher

• BORN: 3/1/1988

• PLAYED FOR TEAM: 2009 TO 2011

Trevor Cahill threw a fastball that dipped as it neared home plate. In 2010, he won 18 games and was picked to pitch in the **All-Star Game**. In 2011, no one in the AL started more games.

## ANDREW BAILEY Pitcher

• BORN: 5/31/1984 • PLAYED FOR TEAM: 2009 TO 2011

It's unusual for a team to rely on a rookie to finish off close games. But Andrew Bailey had unusual talent. He saved 26 games in his first season with the A's and became one of the league's best relief pitchers.

**LEFT**: Rickey Henderson
**ABOVE**: Dennis Eckersley

# CALLING THE SHOTS

When the A's played in Philadelphia, their manager was Connie Mack. He led the team for 50 years. In fact, he kept the job so long he ended up owning the club! Mack's early teams won with speed and pitching. His later teams were built around power.

When the A's played in Kansas City, a man named Charles Finley bought the team. Like Mack, Finley tried to save money whenever he could. Unlike Mack, Finley was so bossy that he often made his players angry. He told the A's what to do and fined them if they did not listen.

Finley was very picky when it came to selecting a manager. He liked to have a say in decisions made during a game, which often led to arguments with his managers. That didn't stop Finley from hiring some of baseball's best minds—especially after the team moved

**LEFT**: Connie Mack watches the action from the dugout in the early 1900s.
**RIGHT**: Tony La Russa leans on the batting cage before a game.

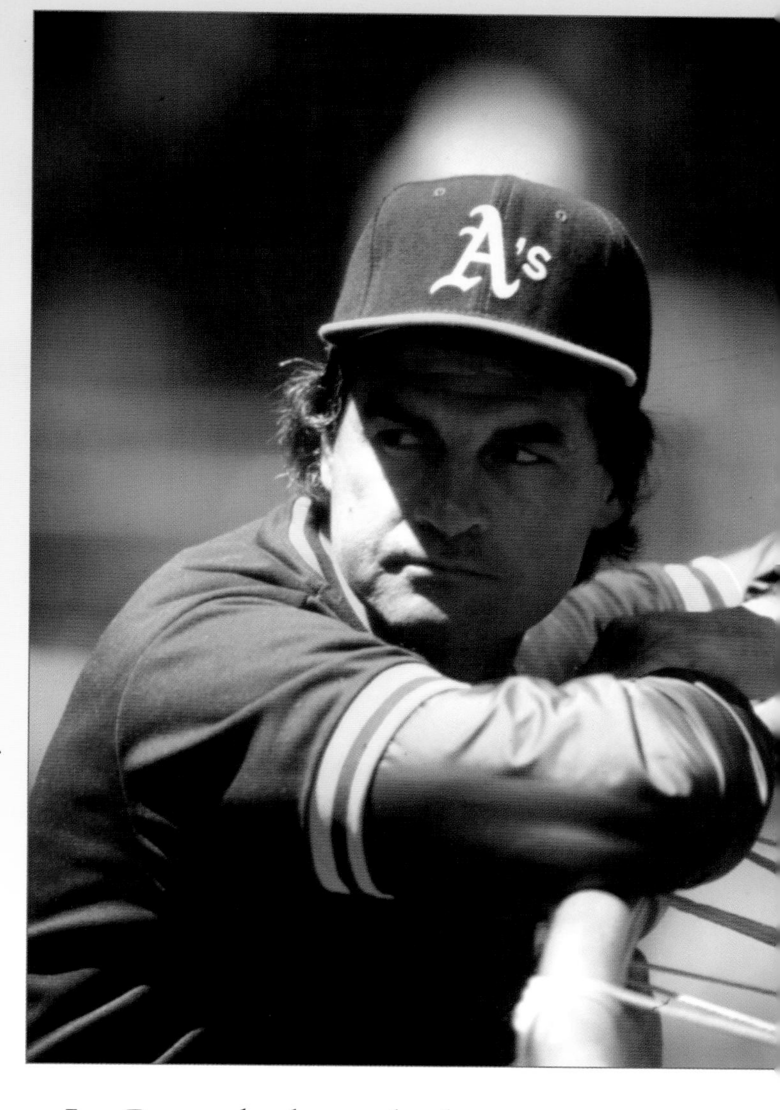


to Oakland. Dick Williams, Alvin Dark, and Billy Martin all led the A's to the **playoffs**. None of them lasted more than three years with the team—they either quit or were fired.

A few years after Finley sold the A's, the team asked one of his old players to manage the club. Tony La Russa had first played for the A's at the age of 18. From 1986 to 1992, Oakland never had a losing record with La Russa in charge. La Russa had good players to work with, but he knew how to get the very best out of them. His knowledge of baseball was unmatched. La Russa led the A's to four AL West titles and three pennants in five years. His accomplishments set the standard for all Oakland managers after him.

# ONE GREAT DAY

No one knew it when the 1971 season began, but the A's were about to make history. That October, they would play in the **postseason** for the first time in 40 years. In July, three A's were invited to play in the All-Star Game: Vida Blue, Dave Duncan, and Reggie Jackson.

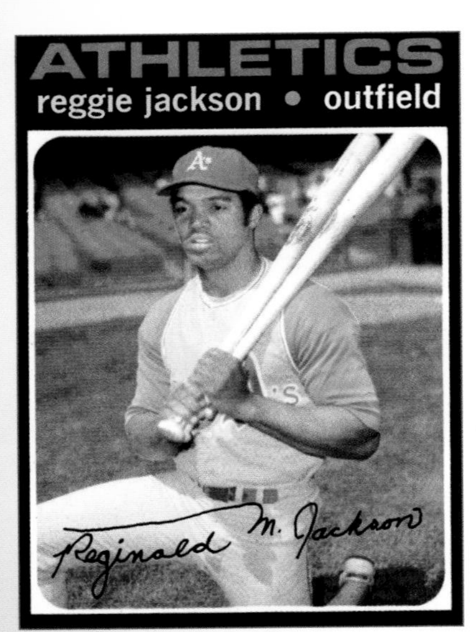


The big story heading into the "Mid-Summer Classic" was that the American League had not beaten the National League since 1962. Blue hoped to change that. He was the starting pitcher for the AL. After three innings, things did not look good. Blue was removed for a pinch-hitter in the bottom of the third inning with his team behind 3–0.

The player selected to hit for Blue was Jackson. With a runner on first base, Dock Ellis threw him a fastball. Jackson put everything he

LEFT: Reggie Jackson poses for his 1971 trading card.
RIGHT: The program from the 1971 All-Star Game is highly prized by A's fans.

had into the swing. The ball jumped off his bat. The outfielders didn't move—they just watched it as it kept rising higher and higher. Jackson himself stood near home plate. He had never hit a ball harder.

The soaring drive looked like it would sail right out of the stadium. The only thing that kept it from flying over the roof was a light tower. The ball had traveled more than 500 feet when it clanked off the metal structure and bounced back on the field. Ernie Harwell, the Detroit Tigers' broadcaster, had watched hundreds of home runs in that stadium. He said Jackson's ball was the hardest hit he'd ever seen.

The home run began a rally by the American Leaguers that helped them take the lead. They won the game 6–4 and ended their eight-year losing streak. "When I hit that one I knew it was out of the ballpark," Jackson said with a smile after the game. "I got all of it."

# LEGEND HAS IT

## WHO WAS CONNIE MACK'S FAVORITE PLAYER?

**LEGEND HAS IT** that Chief Bender was. The A's had many Hall of Fame players in Mack's 50 years as manager, but Bender was his favorite. Bender tied batters into knots with his great curveball and **change-up**. "If I had all the men I've ever handled and they were in their prime," said Mack, "and there was one game I wanted to win above all others, Chief would be my man."

**ABOVE**: Charles "Chief" Bender

**LEGEND HAS IT** that Charles Finley was. In 1964, Finley promised the fans back home that the Beatles would come to Kansas City for a concert. He flew all over the country trying to chase down the British singing group. Finley finally got the Beatles by paying them three times their usual fee. In the 1970s, Finley saw an 11-year-old boy named Stanley Burrell dancing in the parking lot of the Oakland Coliseum and hired him to work for the team. Reggie Jackson nicknamed him "Hammer." Many years later, Burrell hit the music scene as rap star M.C. Hammer.

## HOW DID A WHITE ELEPHANT BECOME THE TEAM'S MASCOT?

**LEGEND HAS IT** that John McGraw was responsible. McGraw was the manager of the New York Giants. During the 1905 season, he was asked what he thought of the A's, since there was a good chance the two teams would meet in the World Series. McGraw called the A's "white elephants," which was a way of saying that they were not as good as they looked. Connie Mack was not insulted. In fact, he decided to make the white elephant a symbol for the team. Before the first game of the World Series, Mack handed McGraw a toy elephant. They both had a good laugh.

# IT REALLY HAPPENED

Back in the early 1900s, when games were often won with bunts and baserunning, a home run was a remarkable thing in baseball. Few players tried to hit the ball out of the park, and even fewer were actually able to do it. In 1911, Frank Baker was the AL's home run champion. The Philadelphia star hit a total of 11 long balls.

That season, Baker saved his best for the World Series. The A's faced the New York Giants, a team with many of baseball's toughest pitchers. Fans everywhere expected a thrilling series.

In Game 2, Baker came to bat against Rube Marquard in the sixth inning with the score tied 1–1 and a runner on second base. Fans were on the edges of their seats. Marquard threw a ball high and

**LEFT**: Fans line up to buy tickets for the 1911 World Series.
**RIGHT**: After the 1911 World Series, the name "Frank" all but disappeared from Baker's baseball cards.

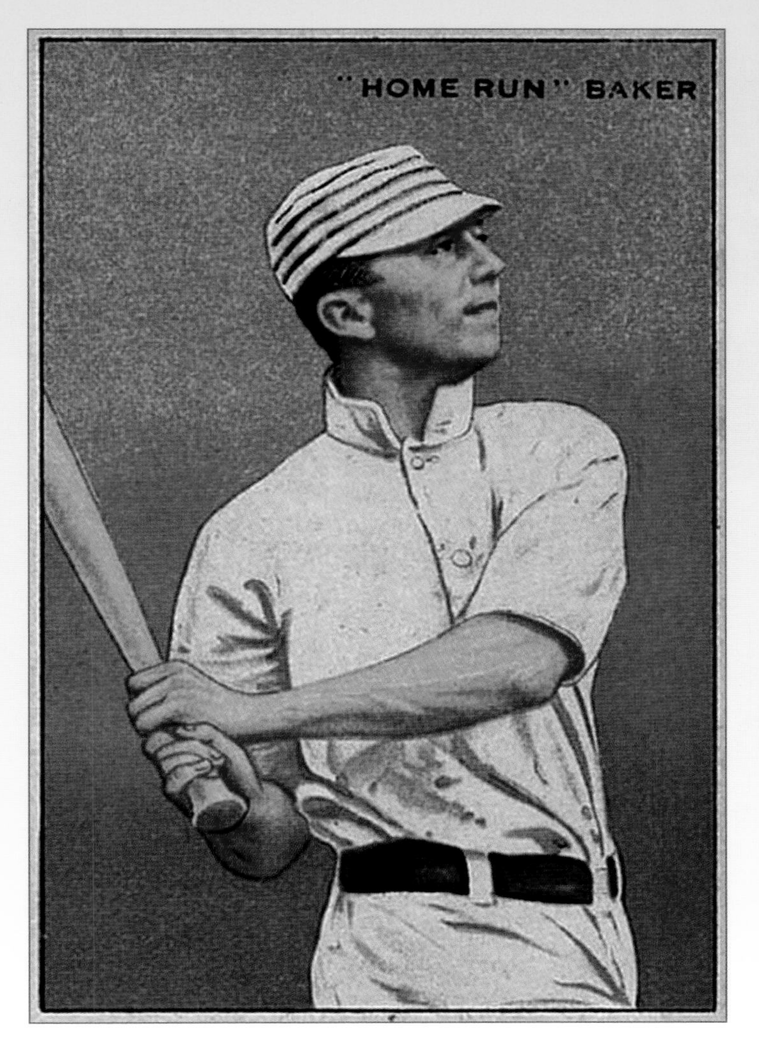


inside, and Baker leaned back and clubbed it. The soaring drive sailed over the fence to give the A's a 3–1 victory.

Game 3 was another nail-biter. With the A's trailing 1–0 in the ninth inning, Baker came to bat against Christy Mathewson. The Giants ace threw his famous "fadeaway" pitch, which curved away from Baker. The slugger was ready. He slammed the ball over the fence to tie the game. The A's won in extra innings.

Feeling they could not lose, the A's went on to win the World Series. Their fans celebrated wildly and could not stop talking about the amazing display of power they had witnessed. From that day on, their World Series hero was known as "Home Run" Baker.

A's

HENDERSON
24

# TEAM SPIRIT

The A's have always had a very personal connection to their fans. In fact, it is safe to say that no team "looks" more like the people who root for them than the A's. Until the players put on their uniforms, it can be hard to tell them apart from the fans.

This ***tradition*** started in the 1970s. Back then, long hair, sideburns, and moustaches were the style. The A's encouraged their players to follow the fashion of the day. Some players were even paid to do so! Rollie Fingers is still famous for his handlebar moustache all these years later. Players such as Dennis Eckersley, Jason Giambi, and Nick Swisher continued this tradition.

CARNEY LANSFORD
OAKLAND A'S

**LEFT**: Rickey Henderson waves to the hometown crowd. The A's have always had a special bond with their fans.
**ABOVE**: Carney Lansford sports a beard and moustache on this mid-1980s A's collector button.

# TIMELINE

This sticker is from the team's time in Kansas City.

**1901**
The A's play their first season.

**1910**
The A's win their first World Series.

**1931**
Lefty Grove wins 31 games.

**1950**
Connie Mack manages the A's for his 50th and final season.

**1955**
The A's move to Kansas City.

The 1910 champions pose for a team photo. Connie Mack is in street clothes.

Rickey Henderson

**1968**
The A's move to Oakland.

**1974**
The A's win their third World Series in a row.

**1982**
Rickey Henderson sets a record with 130 stolen bases.

**1989**
The A's win their ninth World Series.

**2006**
Eric Chavez wins his sixth **Gold Glove** in a row.

**2009**
Andrew Bailey is named AL Rookie of the Year.

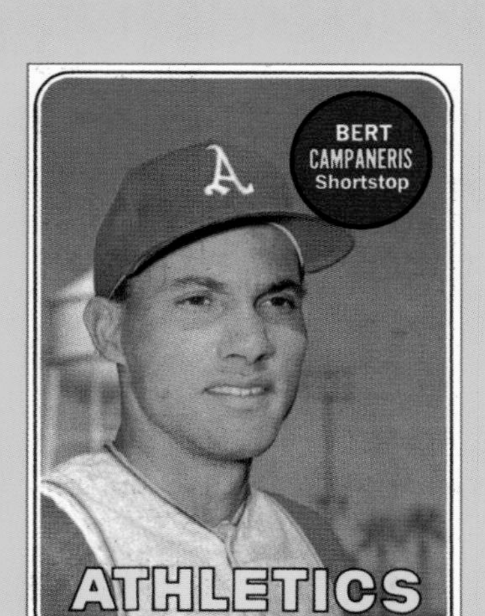


Bert Campaneris led the AL with 62 stolen bases in 1968.

Dave Stewart won 21 games for the 1989 A's.

# FUN FACTS

## NOT-SO-OLD SATCH

In 1965, the A's asked 59-year-old Satchel Paige to pitch an inning against the Boston Red Sox as a ***publicity stunt***. Paige stayed in the game for three innings and did not give up a run.

## FOR YOU, MOM

Dallas Braden pitched a perfect game—27 batters, 27 outs—for the A's on Mother's Day in 2010. He dedicated the game to his own mother, who had died of cancer when he was in high school.

## TENACE ANYONE?

When the A's beat the Cincinnati Reds in the 1972 World Series, only one Oakland player drove in more than one run. Gene Tenace—a backup catcher much of the year—had four home runs and nine RBIs!

## NEVER COUNT THEM OUT

In Game 4 of the 1929 World Series, the A's scored 10 runs in the seventh inning after falling behind 8–0. Their 10–8 victory was the greatest comeback ever in postseason play.

## SUPERSTARS

In 1928, the A's had seven future Hall of Famers on their team: Ty Cobb, Mickey Cochrane, Jimmie Foxx, Lefty Grove, Eddie Collins, Al Simmons, and Tris Speaker.

## DYNAMIC DUO

In 1952, the A's had their last winning season in Philadelphia. That year Bobby Shantz led the AL with 24 wins, and Ferris Fain was the league's top hitter with a .327 average.

## PICTURE THIS

The A's have always liked players who know how to draw a walk. During the 1920s and 1930s, Max Bishop was one of the best. His teammates called him "Camera Eye" because he was so good at judging pitches.

**LEFT**: Gene Tenace
**ABOVE**: Ferris Fain

# Talking Baseball

"A baseball swing is a very finely tuned instrument. It is repetition, and more repetition, then a little more after that."

► ***Reggie Jackson**, on what it takes to be a great hitter*

"Sometimes in this game it's as good to be lucky as it is to be good."

► ***Vida Blue**, on the role that luck plays for a winning team*

"No matter what I talk about, I always get back to baseball."

► ***Connie Mack**, on the sport that he loved*

"If my uniform doesn't get dirty, I haven't done anything in the baseball game."

► ***Rickey Henderson**, on giving his best every time he took the field*

"More important than personal awards is winning the World Series. That's the max that anyone could ask for."

**DENNIS ECKERSLEY**, *ON OAKLAND'S 1989 CHAMPIONSHIP*

"Sweat plus ***sacrifice*** equals success."

**CHARLES FINLEY**, *ON BUILDING A WINNING TEAM*

"I'm too busy having fun to be mean or nasty."

**JASON GIAMBI**, *ON WHY HE'S ALWAYS SMILING*

"I've wanted to do this my whole life, and that desire has never ***wavered.***"

**BARRY ZITO**, *ON PITCHING IN THE BIG LEAGUES*

**LEFT**: Vida Blue
**RIGHT**: Jason Giambi

# GREAT DEBATES

People who root for the Athletics love to compare their favorite moments, teams, and players. Some debates have been going on for years! How would you settle these classic baseball arguments?

### CATFISH HUNTER WAS THE A'S GREATEST PITCHER ...

... because the team could count on him to win 20 games year in and year out. From 1971 to 1974, Hunter (LEFT) went 88–35. During those years, he also went 7–1 in the playoffs and World Series. Even though Hunter was a starter, he even got a save in the 1974 World Series. In his final season with the A's, Hunter won 25 games and was named the Cy Young Award winner.

### CATFISH MAY HAVE BEEN THE BEST 'RIGHTY,' BUT LEFTY GROVE WAS THE BEST EVER ...

... because he just blew batters away. Opposing hitters knew his fastball was coming, and they couldn't touch it. Grove led the AL in strikeouts in seven of his nine seasons with the A's, and was the league's top winner four times. Oh, and when it came to saves, Lefty wasn't bad, either. In 1930, he led all of baseball with nine.

## THE 1970s A'S WOULD HAVE BEATEN THE A'S OF THE 1930s ...

... because everyone on the team knew his job and did it well. Hitters such as Reggie Jackson, Joe Rudi (RIGHT), Sal Bando, and Gene Tenace were at their best under pressure. Bert Campaneris and Bill North energized the club with their baserunning. The starting pitchers were awesome, and the Oakland **bullpen** was the best in baseball. The A's were also a very tough team. They needed to be in order to win the World Series three years in a row.

## TOUGH? NO ONE WAS TOUGHER THAN THE 1930s A'S ...

... because they were fighting for their lives every day. The country was in the middle of the ***Great Depression.*** People everywhere were out of work and desperate for food. The players on the A's felt this pressure, but they still managed to win the World Series twice. Their manager, Connie Mack, may have been the nicest man in baseball, but his players could be scary. What would you expect with nicknames such as Mule, Moose, Black Mike, and The Beast?

# FOR THE RECORD

The great A's teams and players have left their marks on the record books. These are the "best of the best" …

| WINNER | AWARD | YEAR |
|---|---|---|
| Lefty Grove | Most Valuable Player | 1931 |
| Jimmie Foxx | Most Valuable Player | 1932 |
| Jimmie Foxx | Most Valuable Player | 1933 |
| Harry Byrd | Rookie of the Year | 1952 |
| Bobby Shantz | Most Valuable Player | 1952 |
| Vida Blue | Most Valuable Player | 1971 |
| Vida Blue | Cy Young Award | 1971 |
| Gene Tenace | World Series MVP | 1972 |
| Reggie Jackson | Most Valuable Player | 1973 |
| Reggie Jackson | World Series MVP | 1973 |
| Catfish Hunter | Cy Young Award | 1974 |
| Rollie Fingers | World Series MVP | 1974 |
| Jose Canseco | Rookie of the Year | 1986 |
| Mark McGwire | Rookie of the Year | 1987 |
| Terry Steinbach | All-Star Game MVP | 1988 |
| Tony La Russa | Manager of the Year | 1988 |
| Walt Weiss | Rookie of the Year | 1988 |
| Jose Canseco | Most Valuable Player | 1988 |
| Dave Stewart | World Series MVP | 1989 |
| Rickey Henderson | Most Valuable Player | 1990 |
| Bob Welch | Cy Young Award | 1990 |
| Tony La Russa | Manager of the Year | 1992 |
| Dennis Eckersley | Most Valuable Player | 1992 |
| Dennis Eckersley | Cy Young Award | 1992 |
| Ben Grieve | Rookie of the Year | 1998 |
| Jason Giambi | Most Valuable Player | 2000 |
| Miguel Tejada | Most Valuable Player | 2002 |
| Barry Zito | Cy Young Award | 2002 |
| Bobby Crosby | Rookie of the Year | 2004 |
| Huston Street | Rookie of the Year | 2005 |
| Andrew Bailey | Rookie of the Year | 2009 |

Bobby Shantz

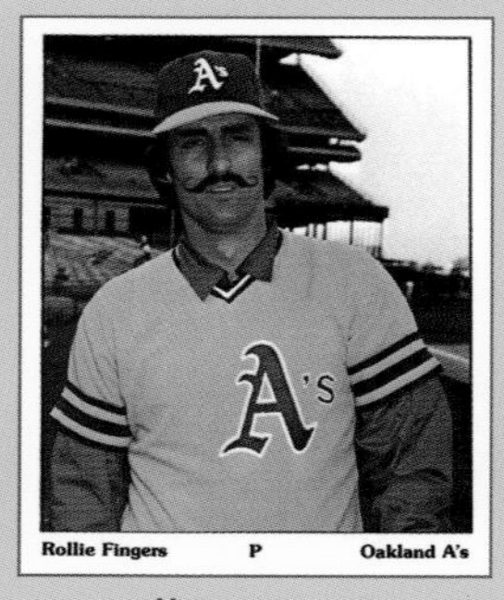

Rollie Fingers

## A'S ACHIEVEMENTS

| ACHIEVEMENT | YEAR |
|---|---|
| AL Pennant Winners | 1902 |
| AL Pennant Winners | 1905 |
| AL Pennant Winners | 1910 |
| World Series Champions | 1910 |
| AL Pennant Winners | 1911 |
| World Series Champions | 1911 |
| AL Pennant Winners | 1913 |
| World Series Champions | 1913 |
| AL Pennant Winners | 1914 |
| AL Pennant Winners | 1929 |
| World Series Champions | 1929 |
| AL Pennant Winners | 1930 |
| World Series Champions | 1930 |
| AL Pennant Winners | 1931 |
| AL West Champions | 1971 |
| AL West Champions | 1972 |
| AL Pennant Winners | 1972 |
| World Series Champions | 1972 |
| AL West Champions | 1973 |
| AL Pennant Winners | 1973 |
| World Series Champions | 1973 |
| AL West Champions | 1974 |
| AL Pennant Winners | 1974 |
| World Series Champions | 1974 |
| AL West Champions | 1975 |
| AL West First-Half Champions* | 1981 |
| AL West Champions | 1988 |
| AL Pennant Winners | 1988 |
| AL West Champions | 1989 |
| AL Pennant Winners | 1989 |
| World Series Champions | 1989 |
| AL West Champions | 1990 |
| AL Pennant Winners | 1990 |
| AL West Champions | 1992 |
| AL West Champions | 2000 |
| AL West Champions | 2002 |
| AL West Champions | 2003 |
| AL West Champions | 2006 |

** The 1981 season was played with first-half and second-half division winners.*

**ABOVE**: Bob Welch
**BELOW**: Eddie Collins led the A's to four pennants from 1910 to 1914.

# PINPOINTS

The history of a baseball team is made up of many smaller stories. These stories take place all over the map—not just in the city a team calls "home." Match the pushpins on these maps to the **TEAM FACTS**, and you will begin to see the story of the A's unfold!

# TEAM FACTS

**1** Oakland, California—*The A's have played here since 1968.*
**2** Pryor, Oklahoma—*Bob Johnson was born here.*
**3** Cincinnati, Ohio—*The A's won the 1972 World Series here.*
**4** Mansfield, Louisiana—*Vida Blue was born here.*
**5** Kansas City, Missouri—*The A's played here from 1955 to 1967.*
**6** Chicago, Illinois—*The A's won the 1910 World Series here.*
**7** Milwaukee, Wisconsin—*Al Simmons was born here.*
**8** East Brookfield, Massachusetts—*Connie Mack was born here.*
**9** Philadelphia, Pennsylvania—*The A's played here from 1901 to 1954.*
**10** Lonaconing, Maryland—*Lefty Grove was born here.*
**11** Pueblo Nuevo, Cuba—*Bert Campaneris was born here.*
**12** Bani, Dominican Republic—*Miguel Tejada was born here.*

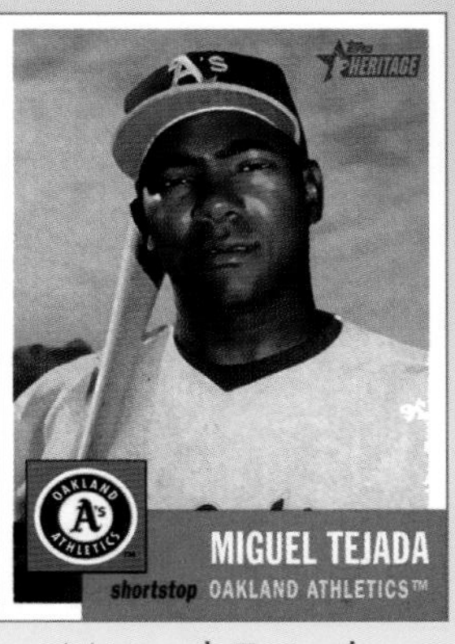

Miguel Tejada

# GLOSSARY

BASEBALL WORDS
VOCABULARY WORDS

**AL WEST**—A group of American League teams that play in the western part of the country.

**ALL-STAR GAME**—Baseball's annual game featuring the best players from the American League and National League.

**AMERICAN LEAGUE (AL)**—One of baseball's two major leagues; the AL began play in 1901.

**BULLPEN**—The area where a team's relief pitchers warm up. This word also describes the group of relief pitchers in this area.

**CHANGE-UP**—A slow pitch disguised to look like a fastball.

**CY YOUNG AWARD**— The award given each year to each league's best pitcher.

***DYNASTY***—A family, group, or team that maintains power over time.

**EARNED RUN AVERAGE (ERA)**—A statistic that measures how many runs a pitcher gives up for every nine innings he pitches.

**FEDERAL LEAGUE**—A third major league that played two seasons, 1914 and 1915.

**GOLD GLOVE** —The award given each year to baseball's best fielders.

***GREAT DEPRESSION***—The economic crisis that started in 1929 and lasted until the 1940s.

**HALL OF FAME**— The museum in Cooperstown, New York, where baseball's greatest players are honored.

***LOGO***—A symbol or design that represents a company or team.

**MOST VALUABLE PLAYER (MVP)**—The award given each year to each league's top player; an MVP is also selected for the World Series and the All-Star Game.

**PENNANT**—A league championship. The term comes from the triangular flag awarded to each season's champion, beginning in the 1870s.

**PLAYOFFS**—The games played after the regular season to determine which teams will advance to the World Series.

**POSTSEASON**—The games played after the regular season, including the playoffs and World Series.

***PUBLICITY STUNT***—Something unusual done to attract people's attention.

**ROOKIE**—A player in his first season.

**RUNS BATTED IN (RBIs)**—A statistic that counts the number of runners a batter drives home.

***SACRIFICE***—Something given up to make an improvement.

**SAVES**—A statistic that counts the number of times a relief pitcher finishes off a close victory for his team.

**SHUTOUTS**—Games in which one team does not score a run.

***TRADITION***—A belief or custom that is handed down from generation to generation.

***TRADITIONAL***—Done the same way from generation to generation.

**TRIPLE CROWN**—An honor given to a player who leads the league in home runs, batting average, and RBIs.

***UNIQUE***—Special or one of a kind.

***WAVERED***—Weakened or softened.

**WORLD SERIES**—The world championship series played between the American League and National League pennant winners.

# EXTRA INNINGS

**TEAM SPIRIT** introduces a great way to stay up to date with your team! Visit our **EXTRA INNINGS** link and get connected to the latest and greatest updates. **EXTRA INNINGS** serves as a young reader's ticket to an exclusive web page—with more stories, fun facts, team records, and photos of the A's. Content is updated during and after each season. The **EXTRA INNINGS** feature also enables readers to send comments and letters to the author! Log onto:

**www.norwoodhousepress.com/library.aspx**

and click on the tab: **TEAM SPIRIT** to access **EXTRA INNINGS**.

Read all the books in the series to learn more about professional sports. For a complete listing of the baseball, basketball, football, and hockey teams in the **TEAM SPIRIT** series, visit our website at:

**www.norwoodhousepress.com/library.aspx**

## ON THE ROAD

**OAKLAND A'S**
7000 Coliseum Way
Oakland, California 94621
(510) 638-4900
oakland.athletics.mlb.com

**NATIONAL BASEBALL HALL OF FAME AND MUSEUM**
25 Main Street
Cooperstown, New York 13326
(888) 425-5633
www.baseballhalloffame.org

## ON THE BOOKSHELF

To learn more about the sport of baseball, look for these books at your library or bookstore:


- Augustyn, Adam (editor). *The Britannica Guide to Baseball.* New York, NY: Rosen Publishing, 2011.
- Dreier, David. *Baseball: How It Works.* North Mankato, MN: Capstone Press, 2010.
- Stewart, Mark. *Ultimate 10: Baseball.* New York, NY: Gareth Stevens Publishing, 2009.

# INDEX

PAGE NUMBERS IN **BOLD** REFER TO ILLUSTRATIONS.



## ABOUT THE AUTHOR

**MARK STEWART** has written more than 50 books on baseball and over 150 sports books for kids. He grew up in New York City during the 1960s rooting for the Yankees and Mets, and was lucky enough to meet players from both teams. Mark comes from a family of writers. His grandfather was Sunday Editor of *The New York Times,* and his mother was Articles Editor of *Ladies' Home Journal* and *McCall's.* Mark has profiled hundreds of athletes over the past 25 years. He has also written several books about his native New York and New Jersey, his home today. Mark is a graduate of Duke University, with a degree in history. He lives and works in a home overlooking Sandy Hook, New Jersey. You can contact Mark through the Norwood House Press website.